# THE NSA CORE – DEEP STATE

# A NOVEL BY JOHNNY PAGE

The NSA Core - Deep State

Written by Johnny Page

This is a work of fiction. Names, characters, places, incidents, and historical events either are the product of the author's imagination or are used fictitiously; and any resemblance to actual persons, living or dead, businesses, companies, events, or locales is entirely coincidental.

All rights reserved. No part of this book may be reproduced, scanned, or distributed in any printed or electronic form without permission of the author.

Copyright © 2023 by Johnny Page

Published by Solitas LLC: Taos, New Mexico

ISBN: 979-8-8528-8400-8
LCCN: 2022908064 (E-book)

Printed in the United States of America

10 9 8 7 6 5 4 3 2 1

# The NSA Core - Deep State

Chapter 1:  Meet the Spooks
Chapter 2:  Amnesia
Chapter 3:  Welcome to The Company
Chapter 4:  Psycho Killer
Chapter 5:  Navy Goons
Chapter 6:  X-Ray Attack
Chapter 7:  Invasion of Privacy
Chapter 8:  New Stasi America
Chapter 9:  John the Ghost
Chapter 10: Patriots versus Tyrants

Prologue:

To the memory of President John F. Kennedy, who was assassinated by the Deep State on November 22, 1963.

Freedom is a fragile thing and is never more than one generation from extinction. -Ronald Reagan

The last hope of human liberty in this world rests on us.
-Thomas Jefferson

Chapter 1 - Meet the Spooks

Liberty cannot be preserved without a general knowledge among the people. -John Adams

In the kingdom of the blind the one-eyed man is king. -Desiderius Erasmus

*****

It all started when I graduated from Arizona Tech. During my last semester towards graduation, a black van started parking around the corner from my place. A strange looking guy started working on the neighborhood telephone box. The black van didn't have the telephone company logo on the door, and it became suspicious after a few days.

This went on for over a month, until my telephone was somehow re-wired to my neighbor. My neighbor, a Vietnam veteran, didn't think it was funny. He told me the guy was a "spook" and he was angry about it. He told me the guy was tapping phones for some reason. The black van disappeared the next day. We had to call the real telephone company out to fix our backwards phone lines.

I started looking for a job and sent out my resume. Within days, I was hired as a Telephone Technician by a weirdo named Frank. Frank acted like a crack-head and appeared to be high on some sort of drug. I would later find out Frank was working for a porn company, and he hired me to install phones and network equipment for them.

This went on for about two weeks, but Frank had no real work for me to do. I would show up for work and there was nothing for me to do. One day, he said he knew some people who have a "Switch" and need someone to run it. He led me downstairs to Telcore USA, where the secretary led me into the switch-room.

There I met Clint Franco and the NSA. First off, Clint told me he was a Navy SEAL. I nodded respectfully. He asked if I knew what the Switch was? I said it was an ESS, or Electronic Switching System, as I'd learned in Telecommunications Electronics at Arizona Tech. "Good," he said, "Because we need someone to run it for us."

Clint then introduced me to Mr. Cozolli, a fat New Yorker, who immediately hired me. I shook his hand and expected some job interview questions, but there were none. Clint didn't ask me a single job interview question either. They both just hired me the minute I met them.

I asked them how much I was going to make? Clint laughed at me, "You don't even have a resume." I was now in charge of a $250,000 telephone-switching system. I looked at the ESS and laughed.

That was easy, I thought. It was the shortest job interview of my life. Of course, they already knew who I was. The NSA recruitment process is simple at best.

The next day Clint introduced me to his friend, Max Hess. Max was a scary-looking German, about 6-foot-5 and 350-pounds. He told me he'd worked for the NSA, CIA, and DEA. He then laughed and described what it's like to shoot someone in a Central American jungle.

I smiled to myself, thinking he was joking. He went on to explain that he was a demolition expert and that, "Clint builds them and I destroy them." Interesting people to work for, I thought to myself. "These telephone switches are more powerful than you think," he told me seriously.

Over the next few weeks, Max began discussions about Hitler and other odd topics. "You wouldn't believe what Uncle Sam used to do," he laughed one day, "You wouldn't believe what Uncle Sam still does."

Later that day, he reviewed my facial features and quietly told Clint, "He's like us." Max, Clint, and I all had blonde hair and blue eyes. I then realized he was a Nazi. A US government Nazi, that is.

Max told me other stories about how his NSA friend worked at a major telephone switching-center. He said his friend took down the entire long distance calling system in Florida with a few commands from a keyboard.

Max looked at me and laughed. He said his friend was owed overtime from "The Company", and had gotten even with them. I shook my head, not knowing. I slowly got to know Clint and Max, and they were becoming friends.

It was funny to watch Max threaten Clint, a Navy SEAL, who I'm sure could have wasted him in a fight. Max was bigger than

Clint, but Clint was a Navy SEAL. Still, Max would shove Clint around like he was the boss.

They would get into small-time fights, with Max pushing Clint around. "I'll snap your neck in one half second," Clint told Max one day. "OK, boss," Max said and backed off.

Clint and others like him showed me how the NSA is working overtime, putting its people (as spies and pawns) into every corner of American life. But, Clint had a strange fear in his eyes, which I wondered about? I couldn't imagine a Navy SEAL fearing anything?

Years later, I would learn (inside the NSA Core) why Clint had a strange fear in his eyes. It wasn't fear at all -- Clint was being spied upon by some very powerful NSA technology. Clint was working inside the NSA Core.

Every day around 4:00 PM, Clint and the other employees would start drinking beer. For a new company starting out, I began to wonder. The company website described my new boss:

Mr. Franco is CTO of Telcore USA and has operated several telecommunications companies. At Spiers Networks he designed and built fiber optic voice and data networks. At GeoSat he installed satellite technology systems. His clients have included: [CENSORED], US Navy, NSA, CIA, DEA, and several foreign governments.

The next day, Clint taught me how to wire-up T1 phone lines into the switch. He said he had a BSEE (Electrical Engineering) degree, which impressed me, since I was graduating with an ASTE (Telecommunications Electronics) degree.

Clint showed me his $50,000 spectrum analyzer, which he said could find a fault between Los Angeles and New York City -- Down to a foot. He also showed me the T3 they were installing, and the CSU/DSU unit.

Clint went on with this tour, and said their $50,000 Web Servers were state-of-the-art. He gave me the keys to the servers and said, "We need you to connect the switch to the servers."

"Sure, no problem," I said. I looked around the switch-room. Look at all this equipment, I thought to myself. What a great job opportunity I have here . . . I'm sure glad I went to Arizona Tech!

Clint then introduced me to Hans Hausen, the CEO of Telcore USA. He was about 75, and the most stressed-out person I've ever met. He appeared crazy in his office, and looked like he had a gun to his head. High blood-pressure, I thought to myself.

Like Clint, Hans had the same strange fear in his eyes. What are these people so afraid of, I wondered? Why is Hans Hausen so stressed-out? He looks like his head is about to explode?

Hans was not very friendly towards me, and he was talking to two 75-year-olds from Dallas, who were selling him Apollo moon-landing photos from the 1970's. They were laughing and pointing at the photos with him for some reason.

It appeared to be an inside joke, which I didn't understand. Hans interrupted them and said, "Welcome to Telcore USA." "Thanks, Mr. Hausen," I replied. "Clint has some work for you to do," he said back.

As weeks went by, I learned more about Telcore USA, and they were learning more about me. One day, while I was working on the servers, Max said out of the blue, "You know how those millionaire's are." That's strange, I thought, because my Dad's a millionaire. "They cut costs all the time," Max said. "Yeah, I know what you mean," I answered.

A few days later Hans started a conversation, explaining that he was a pilot. I told him my Dad is also a pilot, and we talked about landing planes. Hans said he had a small plane out at the airport. That's funny, I thought, because my Dad also has a small plane parked at the airport.

One week, during lunch, Max told me about "Hitler's Revenge", and how the Nazi's infiltrated the US government after World War II. He explained how the Nazi's never lost the war, but relocated to South America.

He said they helped America win the Cold War. He also taught me how to pronounce Dönitz correctly (that's Karl Dönitz, the successor to Hitler). Max went on about U-boats, and how the Nazi's used them to escape from Europe in 1945.

He told me the NSA and CIA have secret agreements to work with Nazis in South America, to fight communism in the West. "Ever heard of Werner von Braun?" Max asked me.

I started to like Max and Clint, but Max was a sinister person. He looked evil and was scary to be around. I knew he wasn't lying about shooting someone in a Central American jungle, and his eyes gleaned when he told me that. Max was the real deal: A US government Nazi.

I wondered what stories he had to tell about his time in Central America, but then again Max was not the kind of person to go out drinking with. Clint, in contrast to Max, was a total professional. He seemed friendly, unlike Max, and yet he was super-confident.

One morning Max came into work with huge black-rings around his eyes from drinking coffee. I hadn't seen him for three weeks. He told Clint he'd signed-up 500 people for Telcore's new ISP service they were selling. He appeared fanatical about it.

Later that day, I met Max's friend, Günter. Günter said he was from Sweden, and that he was going to program the billing/ticketing system for the switch. He told me how he hated Windows, and would be using Linux instead. These people are smart, I thought to myself.

I started to know the rest of the people at Telcore. Bruny Cozolli was a NYSE investment expert and former manager of New York Coast Bank. One day, I found him printing a forty-page securities document for Telcore. I started reading it, and it was a stock offering to investors for Telcore . . . They were selling Telcore stock.

I also met Mr. Dillinger, who was a former Hollywood Movies manager from Los Angeles. He was some sort of marketing expert, and I overheard his plans for Telcore to "wire-up" a new hotel near the Phoenix airport. Clint later explained the technical details and how we would have satellite uplinks, TV-studios -- And how, "Every room would be wired by us."

When I was working on Mr. Dillinger's computer, I noticed plans for something called "Spook Kids TV" on his desk. This was a plan for a new cable TV channel for kids, run by the government. Jesus, I thought . . . They're running a porn company upstairs, and also starting a cartoon channel for kids?

The same day, Bruny told me Hans was from Galveston, and how he'd made his fortune in the oil business. I'd noticed Mr. Hausen's new Mercedes-Benz convertible in the parking lot. It was the most expensive one they sell. Is this the NSA, I wondered?

Clint continued teaching me telephony, and more about the switch. He taught me how to remove the ANI (Automatic Number Identification) sequence from phone calls. Without the ANI, we could make calls anywhere on the planet with no tracing or billing/ticketing. Not only free phone calls, but totally anonymous -- Even from foreign governments.

I then noticed how all the Telcore USA telecommunications equipment had bright orange stickers saying: Property of Bank of South America. Even Clint's spectrum analyzer was owned by the Bank of South America.

Clint laughed when I asked him about this. He then looked at me coldly and said, "Just do as you're told." "And don't ask questions about The Company," he said seriously.

I heard many other odd conversations over the next few weeks at Telcore. A group of investors toured our facilities, and one of them asked Clint what we were doing way-out in a suburb of Phoenix?

"Why isn't Telcore in the downtown central-switching building?" the investor asked him. Clint laughed at him, "If they put one more switch in there, the building will collapse."

The next day Clint hired a Navy goon to do the wiring for our new Phoenix hotel project. Clint told him, "You're former Navy . . . The job's for you, but just don't take too much of a cut." Too much of a cut, I thought? Clint's no businessman -- He's military also. Just what kind of company is Telcore?

Many other odd conversations occurred, like when an 85-year-old from Florida arrived . . . Dr. Falken. Dr. Falken looked like he was 100 years old, with his face all shriveled-up. He met with Mr. Dillinger in our switch-control office. I overheard the entire meeting while I was working on the servers and the switch.

They were drawing diagrams and talking of their proposed "Spook Kids TV" channel. Dr. Falken said the "artists" were finalizing the "programming" for the kids. Mr. Dillinger joked about, "An entire generation," of kids being exposed to their cable channel. What kind of cartoons are these, I wondered? They were talking about "recalls", "implants", and "reinforcement-ratios".

I started noticing other strange things at Telcore. Like how there was no real work to be done. For several weeks, Clint basically had nothing for me to do. I also noticed he started drinking around 1:00 PM instead of 4:00 PM. What a great job, I thought, being paid to drink beer. But, it was getting boring fast.

I spent my days roaming around looking for work to do. I read every technical manual I could find over and over, just to waste time. Finally, I started drinking at 1:00 PM like Clint. I kept asking Clint for jobs to do, and he just said, "Wait and be silent."

Clint was bored also, and he started turning our switch-control office into a high-tech control center. He brought in saws and drills and started building desks and shelves. He put in a refrigerator for ice-cold beer. He started ordering deli sandwiches and beer deliveries for the fridge. He loaded up the fridge with food and beer.

"We should put a locked-door on the switch-room," I told him, "For security reasons." Clint liked the idea and said he was going to put bullet-proof glass around our office and the switch. "Those crack-heads out on the street aren't getting in here," he said, looking out the window to the street. "The ESS is high-tech property and they'd like to get in here."

I sensed Clint didn't like the other employees or Telcore corporate bullshit. So, we started keeping Telcore people locked-out of the switch-room. We even installed an intercom to the secretary up front to keep people out, and it worked. The other employees had to ask permission to enter the switch-room.

Around this time, Telcore went public. They invited me and my girlfriend to their corporate party in downtown Phoenix. They were all dressed-up that night for the show, and told me to come for some "networking". I laughed at the invitation, because I had a date that night with my girlfriend, and I always avoid corporate bullshit.

Max Hess looked like a Nazi, dressed in black, with a long trench-coat, and boots to match. The black-rings around his eyes made him look evil. Bruny Cozolli looked like an Italian mobster, with his 1940's suit on, and his New York accent to match.

Hans Hausen looked rich, with his gold and diamonds on display. The Telcore public relations lady was already drunk when they left me behind around 4:00 PM for the party. Goodbye Telcore, I thought to myself.

The next day a package arrived, and I installed the last piece of hardware (a $25,000 circuit board) to complete our T3 installation. Clint said to be careful with it, because it was on loan from his friends, until we could get our own.

The boss from the porn company upstairs watched patiently as I installed it. He looked like he needed the bandwidth badly for his porn business. I installed the board and all lights were green. We were up to full T3 speed in no time.

The next day was Friday and payday, but there were no paychecks for anyone. They said Mr. Hausen had our paychecks, but he was nowhere to be found. The entire staff of Telcore waited until after 7:00 PM, when Hans finally showed up and gave us hand-written checks.

A week later, Clint said they wanted me to go to Miami to attend ESS school. He said it was a two-month long course covering everything a Switch Technician would want to know.

He explained that when Telcore bought the $250,000 ESS, they got the training for free. "Sure," I said, "I'll take a trip to Florida for a few months . . . No problem."

Mr. Cozolli made the travel arrangements, and said they had an economy motel for me to stay at for the two months. He assured me it was a decent place to stay, but he seemed nervous about it for some reason? Whatever, I thought, I could use a vacation after graduating from Arizona Tech.

Clint was the first and last NSA operative I met who garnered respect. Clint was a total professional and Navy SEAL. Clint was a cool dude who liked to drink beer. Over the ensuing years, I would meet the rest of "The Company".

"The Company", a play on words another operative taught me. A secret society of former military, criminals, and other scum working for "The Company" -- Or whatever else you could call it.

Their mantra: "I will deny all knowledge and connection to the Agency." Their silent code is fear of the NSA Core. I would learn this denial and fear defines NSA operatives, as a way of life.

Wives, families, and friends are involved. The NSA is a foreign intelligence service, I wondered? What is the NSA doing in Phoenix spying on Americans and running telecommunications networks? The NSA Charter of 1947 prohibits domestic spying on Americans.

Who are these people, I wondered? From what I could tell, the NSA appeared to be a criminal organization operating domestically in 1999? How did that happen? These questions and more led me further down the road into the NSA Core.

Chapter 2 - Amnesia

Our liberty depends on freedom of the press, and that cannot be limited without being lost. -Thomas Jefferson

We know it's illegal and we're doing it anyways.
-Cyclops (NSA spook)

*****

I arrived in Miami the last week of May, 1999. I'd never been to Florida, and it looked like a giant swamp from the airplane. The trees looked strange and I could see swamps as we flew over Florida. The cute girl at the car rental counter was friendly though, and she welcomed me to Miami.

I drove from the airport and got lost, but eventually found the Floridian motel Mr. Cozolli had arranged. The desk clerk acted strange when I checked in. When I asked him for a room far away from the other rooms (so I could crank up my stereo), he became really nervous. He said he wasn't sure and to ask again tomorrow.

Why was the desk clerk so nervous, I wondered? The parking lot was empty, and I could have moved to any room available. I ordered a pizza and drank some beer, thinking ahead to my ESS training class on Monday morning.

Miami felt like a strange place, but then again I was a stranger in a strange land. I couldn't explain it, but I could feel it. There was something strange about this place. The water tasted horrible and I wasn't used to the humidity either.

I went to the local grocery store and bought some bottled water and food. I drank some more beer and cranked up my stereo, smiling to myself. A vacation is just what I need, I thought to myself. I made some phone calls and went to sleep early.

The next day I asked the desk clerk again for a different room. He again became really nervous, and said to check back again tomorrow. What the fuck, I thought? Why is this desk clerk so nervous? I decided to check out Miami and the local sights that day, and wished my girlfriend was with me.

The next day, on Sunday, I asked him again for a different room. This time the clerk was ready for me, and said he would move me around back, away from the other guests. He still seemed nervous towards me for some reason. The room was a bigger suite, but now I had two neighbors a few doors down.

The first neighbor I noticed had a couple of vicious Dobermans setup in cages on the grass across the parking lot. These were no ordinary Dobermans. They looked like killers. I could tell by the intensity in their eyes that they were serious beasts. They were the most intense dogs I'd ever seen. They looked like trained killers.

There were two guys and one woman who owned them, staying a few doors down. I heard them talking in the parking lot, and they were speaking German. What are these Germans doing in Miami with vicious Dobermans, I wondered?

I also noticed the other neighbor, who was about 85-years-old. He looked like a ghost or something. He was pale white, with gold glasses, gold rings, and a gold watch.

Even his Mercedes-Benz had gold trim. This guy really likes gold, I laughed to myself. I tried to make eye contact with him, but he walked really slowly. He looked like a zombie or something . . . The way he walked. There was something sinister about him, but I couldn't explain it.

I sensed evil from him, but I couldn't explain it. I shook my head, wondering? There was something strange going on at the Floridian motel. This old man was evil, and he was avoiding me. He looked so old and evil!

I drank some beer and went swimming all day long. The next day, I arrived late (as usual) at the ESS training center. The teacher was about 65, and he had a Florida drawl. He talked really fast, like a cartoon character, and handed out our first training book.

He then looked at the ceiling and laughed about how we were being "recorded". He joked about how, "Some of us," were involved with the US government. He went on, and explained that he had nothing to do with it.

On our first break, another student approached me. He was overly friendly, shook my hand, and said his name was Juan. He asked if I was from Arizona? "Yeah," I said. He said he was also from Arizona, and started a conversation about Phoenix. He made some local references, and was obviously eager to become my friend.

After break, the teacher started teaching us every detail of an ESS, and he was actually good. Although it got boring at parts, we would graduate with a fine-tuned education on the ESS. As always, I took detailed notes on every aspect of the technical systems.

The teacher was also funny, and made jokes about Florida's right-to-carry laws. He said he was packing a .45 from hell. Being from Arizona, I was starting to like Florida and its people. The teacher was a *Real American*, carrying a .45 Smith & Wesson.

After class, Juan met me in the parking lot. He asked me if I liked to party? "Sure," I said, and he invited me over to his hotel. He gave me his phone number and asked me for mine. He made a joke about Phoenix, and asked where I got the sports car?

I told him the cute girl at the rental agency gave it to me. He laughed and wondered why he didn't get a sports car also? I laughed and said, "I don't know . . . It's because she was cute and liked me."

The next day in class a new student arrived, and was seated right next to me. He said his name was Dexter, and he was from Waco, Texas. He was ugly and missing teeth, and had a bad Texas accent. At lunch Juan and Dexter got together like friends, and asked me if I wanted to go to lunch with them?

I went to lunch with them and started asking them questions. Juan said he was in the US Navy for eight years. He said he'd gotten out, and was now with "The Company". Dexter said he'd never been in the military, but his Dad was a US Naval Intelligence officer. They were both eager to know me, and we set plans to go out partying that night.

We met at a bar that night in Miami, and started drinking. Both of them acted odd, as if they were on a mission or something. They seemed like they wanted to know me, but had more questions than answers. They weren't too bright.

We hit the strip clubs, and even went bowling. The first thing Juan did was light up a marijuana cigarette and offer it to me. "No, I don't smoke," I said. Dexter laughed and replied, "I don't like it either." But, then Juan and him smoked it in the car and became really quiet.

After hitting some strip clubs, we went bowling. Juan was getting wasted by now, after several hours of drinking. I had my Arizona Tech hat on and he started babbling about high-technology and said, "We give you the best technology in the world." "Oh, yeah?" I looked him in the eye.

He grinned at me, and started talking straight with me for a change. I asked him if he was NSA or CIA? He nodded and said, "I'm with The Company." He looked around the bar and laughed at everyone drunkenly. "We own this state!" he said. "Florida is the CIA's state . . . We own this place!" He laughed again, "We own Florida."

I was getting drunk also at this point, and started questioning Juan about his Navy background. After listening to his stories, I told him the Navy was for gay men. I explained all my friends were in the Army, Air Force, or Marines. I talked about the Marines I'd known, and how they were true patriots.

Juan became angry and got really crazy towards me. He was losing it and I was laughing at him. It was looking like a fight, as I'd planned. Out of the blue, he said he had a "Get out of jail" card from the CIA. He said he could walk away from any jail in Florida -- No questions asked. He was serious about this, and I shook my head.

Like a threat, he told me again, "The CIA owns Florida -- I can walk out of any jail right now." Dexter got up and immediately backed him off, grabbing him by the arm. He took him towards the video game room and calmed him down.

I sat there thinking about punching Juan in the face, but I thought better. I'm a long way from Arizona, I told myself. So, I backed off also. After a few minutes, Dexter and Juan came back to the table. Dexter made a dumb joke about how he wouldn't join the Navy, "For a million dollars." He was grinning at me like he'd sent some sort of message.

For the next week at ESS class, I avoided both of them. When Juan asked for my business card I told him to fuck off. So, is this the NSA, I wondered? No matter, as I focused on my studies -- Learning everything I could about the ESS. I was even thinking of calling Clint Franco about my progress, since I liked him.

Then I returned to my room that day after class, and his wife called me. I was surprised to speak with Clint's wife. I'd never met her, nor even heard about her from Clint. What's even more bizarre is she started asking me technical questions about the ESS, and telephony in general.

I actually got out my telecommunications books to answer her questions about B8ZS protocols and SS7 signaling. The next day Clint called me and said I had, "Done good." He asked me if I was taking notes on the ESS?

I said, "Yes, sir." I told him how I'd asked the teacher about one of the red-lights he was having trouble with on the ESS. Clint couldn't get this one red-light to go out on the ESS, and said he'd try what the teacher recommended. The ESS was a complicated system, he told me.

I now had a new neighbor at the Floridian motel. A blonde whore had moved in next to the Germans, and she was doing lots of business. I noticed her as I was sitting outside, relaxing after class. She had major traffic coming and going about every thirty minutes.

Jesus, I thought, what kind of place am I staying at? I thought of my girlfriend so far away, and I called her up and told her I missed her. I then went swimming. I'd been in Miami about three weeks, and was now used to the humidity and climate. I looked up at the sun, and realized how far I was from Arizona and home.

The next day after class something really strange happened. I was into a routine by this time, and would get back to my room around 3:00 PM. As usual, I returned to the Floridian motel, and tossed my ESS books onto the bed. I wasn't tired at all, and was thinking of drinking beer and going swimming.

Instead, I was immediately knocked-out within minutes of arriving in my room. There's no other way of describing it. I was literally knocked-out within minutes of arriving back from ESS school!

I woke up the next morning around 6:00 AM, with absolutely no memory of what had happened. I was lying on my bed where I'd sat at 3:00 PM the day before, with my clothes on and ESS books next to me.

I tried as hard as I could to recall what had happened, but I was at a loss? From 3:00 PM to 6:00 AM the next morning, I suffered from amnesia. I've never, ever "lost time" in my entire life and I'm 100% healthy. I was drugged and I'm sure of it.

I called up my girlfriend that day and told her what had happened. She said to just ignore the amnesia episode, because it was the last week of ESS school. She told me to just finish my classes and return home to Arizona.

That week our class went on a tour of the ESS factory in Miami. It was part of the package my bosses had paid $250,000 for. Our tour guide, Damien, said he was from Brazil, and told us how he really liked Florida.

His German accent was pronounced, and it was difficult to understand his English. He explained every detail of the ESS assembly and manufacturing process, and he was quite friendly.

That same week Juan and Dexter invited me to an ESS graduation party for our class. While I was reluctant to go, since I didn't want to know them, I said "OK." What the hell, I thought. If anything, I'll punch Juan in the face and get drunk.

Unfortunately, that's exactly what happened. I arrived at the hotel and the party started. Only the guys from our class showed-up, and there were no women at all. We were of course, bored, and then Juan started selling cocaine and marijuana to the other ESS technicians.

Then he cranked up the stereo with some really bad Cuban music. "You got any better music?" I asked him, "Maybe some Rock and Roll?" "No," he said to me, "Do you want some cocaine?" "No, I don't want cocaine from you," I sneered at him. I drew a fist and almost punched him.

One of the other technicians, from Kansas, was also offered cocaine and marijuana from Juan. I'd gotten to know him a bit, and he was from Wichita and was married with kids. Juan started selling him some marijuana, and I interrupted.

"Juan's with the DEA," I told him. "He's a spook . . . He's a goon." "I wouldn't buy a used car off him," I said. "He's setting you up and your family also." "Juan's a government agent."

The guy from Wichita looked at me, then Juan, and refused the sale. He shook his head and became nervous. "It's OK," I told him. "Juan works for the government." "He told me he's with the DEA."

My friend from Kansas looked really nervous, at this point. "It's OK," I reassured him. "These people are goons, and it's about time we started hurting them." I looked at Juan. "Let's go outside, Juan," I said. "It's about time we had a little talk."

Juan became shifty-eyed and yelled, "Fuck you Whitey!" We both went outside onto the walkway of the hotel where he was staying. After some stupid talk, I sucker-punched him in the face! I decked Juan with a single throw! "Get up, you government pig!" I shouted at him.

He was lying on the deck, and I thought of kicking him hard. I backed-off myself, as I'd been in street-fights in Los Angeles before. I wanted to round-house him, but I stopped. I shook my head and walked away. "You stupid government whore!" I shouted at him one last time.

Chapter 3 - Welcome to The Company

I have sworn upon the altar of God, eternal hostility against every form of tyranny over the mind of man.
-Thomas Jefferson

It's the eye of the state and it gives us a God-like view over America. -Birdman (NSA spook)

*****

After graduation from ESS school, I returned to Phoenix and Telcore USA. Clint was happy to see me when I reported back for work. He said he had, "Major work for me to do." He asked me how I liked Miami and I said, "It was kinda strange."

He immediately set me to work programming the Switch for the routing tables we needed. This was the core of ESS operation, and what I'd learned in Miami. My job as Switch Technician was all about routing and tables. While I was in Florida, Telcore had significantly expanded, and they were now on the front-page of the Phoenix newspapers.

They had signed-up thousands of customers while I was gone. Telcore was offering everything from super-fast Internet to dial-up, local, interstate, and international calling. They had a room full of telemarketers selling our services. It looked like a circus to me.

The next day a package arrived at Telcore USA. It said it was from Spicorp from Bethesda, Maryland. The secretary left it for us in the switch-room. I wondered what was in it, but thought I'd wait. Clint was talking about upgrading the Switch, after I'd told him about the ESS school upgrades they sold us.

When I returned from break, Max was back. He was grinning for some reason. He looked like a goon as usual, dressed in a black trench coat with his black boots on. Max was smiling, with huge black rings around his eyes. He looked at Clint, "I signed-up over 500 accounts in the last month," he said.

"That's great," Clint said. "Who did you sign up?" he asked. "All our friends," Max replied, "And then some." Clint laughed, "Good job." Clint rebooted one of our servers and left.

Max asked me how I was and how I liked Miami? "It was kinda strange," I told him like Clint. He then started another conversation about the Nazis. "The Third Reich never died," he told me, "It was all transferred to Argentina."

"OK," I said, "This is America, not the Third Reich." "Why are you always talking to me about the Nazis?" I asked. He looked at me and laughed, "Capitalism and Fascism are best friends . . . Always have been."

I nodded and agreed with him. "You're right about that," I said. "The greatest capitalist in history was Mr. Krupp . . . He eventually owned everything." Max smiled and said, "I know."

Later that day, I noticed what the new package was. Clint had installed it onto the T3. It was feeding off the T3, but I didn't know what it was. I showed it to Max, and asked him what it was? Max looked at me and laughed.

"That's us . . . That's NSA," he said. His eyes lit up, "That's the NSA tap." He shook his head at me, "You sure are green, aren't you?" "Green?" I replied. "That tap feeds every bit and byte to the NSA," he explained. "Didn't they teach you that in school?" he wondered.

About a month later Hans Hausen announced the *Telcore Golf Classic*. This was a golf tournament in Scottsdale run by Telcore. Clint told me former Vice President Theil would be there for Telcore, and that I could meet him. He also said Roger Yuma might show up, and other football stars.

That's really weird, I thought. Telcore was a start-up company less than a year old, and already Vice President Theil was showing up at their golf tournament? What's even stranger is how Roger Yuma was to appear, along with other football stars.

I told Clint I'd be there, along with my girlfriend. "I can't guarantee you'll meet the Vice President," he said. "But, I can guarantee you're with us," he looked at me seriously. "We need Switch Technicians like you more than ever, and you're now part of The Company," Clint said.

"Yes, sir," I said to Clint and saluted him, knowing he was a Navy SEAL. "Cut out the bullshit," he said. "I quit the Navy a long time ago." "I'm NSA now and liking it," he went on. "Whatever I want they send to me, and whatever I need they send to me." "I have unlimited NSA resources," he told me.

He laughed, "It's all bullshit." "I've been with the The

Company for so long . . . It's actually boring," he joked. "Anyways, you can meet the Vice President if you want to," he said, "Or, you can meet Roger Yuma, a real winner, and watch him lose on the golf course."

"What?" I said. "The problem with these quarterbacks is they can't hit a golf ball," Clint laughed. "Golf is a mean game, even for quarterbacks like Yuma," he said. "I can't even hit the damn ball straight." "Yeah," I agreed, "I've played every sport you can think of and golf isn't easy," I replied.

A month after the *Telcore Golf Classic*, Hans Hausen disappeared. No one knew where he was or why his voice mailbox was full of un-answered messages? He owed me a paycheck for three weeks of work, along with the entire staff of Telcore. Hans Hausen disappeared overnight and owed all of us wages and checks for work done.

I later found out that not only Hans Hausen, but Bruny Cozolli both disappeared together at the same time. Clint said they both flew from Phoenix to South America for some reason? He then told me, "It's over," and how Telcore was shutting-down.

Telcore USA turned out to be a million-dollar fraudulent Phoenix telecommunications company. They not only ripped me off for three weeks of wages, but also ripped off investors for millions of dollars.

I saw Clint again about a week later. I looked him in the eyes and said, "Welcome to The Company." Clint thought about it and became angry. "It's all bullshit and you better shut-up about it!"

"Don't fuck with The Company and The Company doesn't fuck with you!" he told me. "Just do as you're told," he looked at me seriously, "And don't ask questions." "OK," I said and left Telcore USA.

Chapter 4 - Psycho Killer

Government is not reason; it is not eloquence; it is force. Like fire, it is a dangerous servant and a fearful master.
-George Washington

We have no moral compass here at the NSA. -Cyspy (NSA spook)

*****

I was lucky to get hired at a new company called MRI Medical. Within ten days of quitting Telcore USA, I had a new job as Electronic Technician with MRI Medical. This was a new challenge for me and I welcomed it.

My education in electronics and circuit analysis paid off, and my new boss seemed to like me a lot. We were dealing with critical medical equipment, used in MRI radiation therapy. This was a major change from Telcore USA.

I had to deal with a factory system: With all the parts, people, and problems. I wasn't working with telecommunications equipment anymore, but medical equipment from now on. I was dealing with serious circuits and medical devices, and I liked it.

My new boss Jim played EE games with me, and tried to make me look stupid in front of the other engineers. He challenged me with real-world circuits and schematics. Of course, I knew the circuit logic and answers to his questions.

After the first week he stopped it, and admitted that I knew what I was doing. He looked at me one day, sure of himself. "Arizona Tech is a good school," he said. "My brother went there and it's an excellent school." "I have a BSEE from Tucson Technical College," he said in a friendly manner.

"Yeah," I replied, "They taught us everything you could want to know about circuit analysis at Arizona Tech." "My teachers taught us Op-Amp design and circuits," I said. "My final exam was the analysis of a nightmare Op-Amp circuit." "Yeah, I can imagine," Jim said.

"We had goons from the military teaching us," I went on. "It was a goddamned nightmare," I told him. Jim laughed, "Arizona Tech goes back to the Cold War," he replied. "I know they worked on Air Force top secret stuff," he said. "My brother said some of the teachers were spooks." "It's a high-tech college," he said and walked away.

With my new job, I had to find a new place to live. MRI Medical was far out from the city of Phoenix, on the edge of the desert and mountains. For months, I searched the small town newspapers near MRI Medical for a place to rent. After about two months, I found a place out in the mountains far away, but close.

After work one night, I checked out the new place for rent. The guy gave me winding directions this way and that, all leading to a driveway with a huge German Coat of Arms sign that read: "Wolf's Lair".

That's when I met Helmut. First off, he said he was from Florida. He looked psychotic and his eyes were black not blue. "You know how us Floridians are," he sneered at me. That's crazy, I thought, thinking of Telcore USA!

I looked around and noticed both cars in the driveway had Florida license plates. "You're a long way from Florida," I laughed at him. "It doesn't matter now does it?" he said. Great, I thought . . . Just my kind of people.

Helmut showed me the huge house for rent for only $500 a month. It had everything, including a hot tub and sauna. What a deal, I thought to myself -- For $500 bucks a month? He said there's no deposit and no lease. That's when I looked him in the eyes. He looked psychotic and his eyes were glazed over, as if he were on drugs.

He started smacking his keys against his leg, in a crazy way. He was smacking his leg, in a stabbing motion! He looked like a psycho killer, with black eyes. His violent key-smacking against his leg was crazy!

This guy is dangerous, I thought to myself. He locked his eyes on me like a mad dog. "It won't take long . . . Maybe a few months," he said with his German accent. He kept smacking his keys against his leg! "You can move in right now," he said.

"OK," I said, "I'll be back tomorrow with the rent." "You know about Florida gators?" Helmut asked. "No, I've never met them," I laughed at him again. "They'll rip you to shreds in the swamps," he snarled at me. "Well, this isn't Florida, is it?" I replied.

I went to my Jeep and grabbed my brand new OZ-18 Pepper Spray bottle. "Ever heard of Gila Monsters?" I asked him. "No," he replied. "They'll bite your leg with poison," I said. I pepper-sprayed the bastard and watched him crawl on the ground like a bug.

"You fucking psycho killer!" I shouted at him. I round-housed him a couple of times with my boots. "Get up you psycho killer!" I shouted. I was about to crush his skull when I thought about how late it was, and how I had to get to work in the morning.

As I drove away, I realized Helmut and the huge house for rent was a NSA set-up to kill me. The bastards were after me and I was sure of it. I started to do some re-thinking the next day at work. I decided to start camping out in the mountains and buy a gun.

I bought a Smith & Wesson .45 the next day for self defense. I spent my next paycheck on camping gear and headed to the mountains with my new gun. I started camping way out in the mountains in the forest trees. I've always liked camping and thought it was fun.

Every day after work, I made sure no one was following me, and I would turn up into the forest to my campsite. My Jeep 4x4 can crawl rocks, and I was just off the main road back to the city. I was totally hidden off the road in the forest trees, and no one knew where my campsite was.

This worked for about a month. Then one night, while I was sleeping in the forest, someone started shouting my name off in the distance. I woke up and heard someone shouting my name! I grabbed my gun and started the Jeep. I drove down from my campsite to the road and found an old Ford truck parked right next to my forest campsite was.

"Fuck You!" I yelled into the dark forest at 2:00 AM and then shot out the tires on the Ford truck. I headed back to the city. That's crazy, I wondered, how did they find me? How did they find me in the forest? No one ever followed me?

Around the same time, MRI Medical hired a new EE for our department. They said he had a MSEE degree. They said he worked in aerospace and used to work for a defense contractor. One of my bosses, a mechanical engineer, said he hired him because of his resume.

What was strange is how he went from the engineering department, into my technician department, and wanted a desk near me in the same room. After setting up a desk in my department, he started saying strange things to me.

I'd barely spoken to him for a week and he said to me, "You know how those Floridians are." I laughed and thought about Helmut, who I'd pepper-sprayed a month before. Is this guy a spook also, I wondered?

He also started talking about telecommunications to me, not the medical equipment we were working on. He asked me if I remembered "switching circuits" and more. My boss Jim told me he was about to get fired because he wasn't working with the other engineers upstairs.

It's like he was put into MRI Medical to be near me and talk to me. Around the same time, I was eating pizza at the same place every day for lunch. One day, a military-looking guy came in and ordered a pizza and sat right next to me inside the restaurant. The place was empty and he sat right next to me.

He started talking on his cell phone and was saying really strange things. "I can't believe you're not dead yet," he said to the other person on the phone. "I can't believe you're not in prison yet," he went on. "The Company needs you," he continued. I got up and left the restaurant and wondered if he was sending me some sort of message?

A few weeks later, I met Jennifer at MRI Medical, and we started going out on dates. Jennifer was a cute blonde with big boobs and she kissed me on our first date. A month or so later, I moved in with her at her apartment in Phoenix. It was love from day one, and she fell over like she was drunk, when I first asker her out.

Then the bad news came to us MRI Medical employees. MRI Medical was closing the factory and we were all losing our jobs. MRI Medical decided to shut-down our factory and move all our jobs to Mexico. Jennifer had just bought a brand new Jeep on payments. Great, I thought, time to get out the resume again.

Chapter 5 - Navy Goons

We are as a people inherently and historically opposed to secret societies, to secret oaths, and to secret proceedings.
-John F. Kennedy

Yo, ho, ho, sir. -Goony (NSA spook)

*****

It was easy for me to get a new job, and I was hired immediately by Radtronics. They interviewed me and hired me while I was still finishing up my work at MRI Medical. Jennifer had no trouble finding a job either, with her Biology degree and career in hospital and medical work.

The new job interview lasted a few minutes with a few questions, and the guy who hired me was not my new boss. It was another incredibly short and easy job interview. When I started my first day at work, I met my new boss.

My new boss turned out to be a slimy Navy goon, about 75-years-old. He had a pig-like face with a pig nose, and a Hitler-style haircut that was greased back. He actually wore hair grease in his hair from the 1940's, I think.

The first thing I noticed was his cubicle was full of Navy junk. He had a toy submarine model on his desk, and a Navy football sitting on his shelf. He had all sorts of other Navy junk all over the place. He also had a BSEE degree hanging on the wall. He was in charge of all the department Electronic Technicians, like me.

He said his name was Herbert, and quickly introduced me to my new co-workers. I first met Beeker and then a woman technician named Boo. They both said they were former Navy, and had spent eight years in the service.

I'd barely met them and for some reason, Beeker started wrapping power cords around in a circle on the floor really fast. He looked like a Navy shipman coiling-up ropes on a ship or something? Great, I thought to myself, more Navy goons.

I suddenly realized the whole job interview was another set-up, and a waste of my time. Another set-up from these NSA psychos! I was angry, to say the least. "Did you follow the checklist?" Boo asked Beeker. "Yes, maam," he replied. "Did you comply with the testing?" she asked him next. "Yes, maam," he answered.

Beeker then showed me what we were working on. It was highly dangerous medical radiation equipment, and I'm sure they both have cancer by now. "Do you wear radiation vests while you work on these machines?" I asked Beeker. "No, we are just very careful with our procedures," he answered.

I read the "Danger! Warning! Caution!" labels on the box they wanted me to work on. Beeker then showed me how to tweak the settings on the box. Jesus, I thought, these Navy technicians are working on incredibly dangerous radiation devices! This is a one-way ticket to the cancer center!

I thought of quitting right then and there, but decided to talk to Jennifer about it first. That night, Jennifer and I had a long talk. I told her about how I met the NSA and told her all about it. She thought it was incredible and she believed every word I said! She said she thinks I'm really smart and maybe they want to hire me really bad.

"Why don't they just leave me alone?" I asked her. "I don't want to work for the NSA or have anything to do with the military or wars." "Are you a pacifist?" she asked. "No, I just don't believe in wars or bombing people on the other side of the planet." She smiled at me and laughed, "I don't either."

After talking with Jennifer that night, I decided to give Radtronics another day before quitting. I went back to work the next morning, and when I walked in the door my new boss Herbert was waiting for me. He said he wanted to talk to me in his cubicle.

He said I did a good job on my first day, and the other technicians liked me. "We don't want to lose you this time," he said strangely. "You seem like a smart technician, and I would like to offer you a raise." "OK," I said calmly. "How much?" I asked. "How much do you want to stay with The Company?" he asked me.

"I want $25 per hour starting today," I said. Herbert raised his eyebrows and shook his head. "Let me talk to my boss about it . . . That's a major pay increase," he answered. "OK," I said and went back to work.

Beeker and Boo looked nervous for some reason when I came

back to work with them. Beeker and Boo both had desks facing me and I had a desk facing them. It was two against one, or maybe one against two?

From the first minute I met them, Boo was always on her computer with a chat-box, reading out loud. She was chatting with her husband or family at work it sounded like?

Beeker was about 5-foot-4 and scrawny without muscles. Boo was about 5-foot-1 and maybe 220 pounds. She was super-fat and was constantly eating at her desk. "Is that your real name, Boo?" I asked her. "No, they started calling me that in the Navy," she replied. "They told me I'm spooky."

Beeker took me on a tour of our department and Radtronics. He showed me the entire factory, and said he used to work as a Navy Radar Technician. "We're you on a ship?" I asked. "Yes, sir, I was on a small Navy ship for a long time," he replied. "I was one of the radar technicians," he said. "Did you serve in the Iraq War?" I asked. "No, sir, I never saw combat," he answered.

After the tour, Herbert called me back into his cubicle. "We can't give you $25 per hour, but we can pay you $20 per hour," he said. "No," I said, "I want $25 per hour because I'm worth it to The Company." Herbert shook his head. "That's more than the other technicians are making and it has to be reasonable," he answered.

"OK," I said, "I'll take $20 per hour starting right now." Herbert agreed, "You're now making $20 per hour as of now . . . Get back to work." I went back to work with Beeker and Boo. Beeker was doing his Navy coil-up the power lines routine, when I came back.

Boo was on her chat-box computer, talking to her family, I guessed? That's when it got weird, really fast. Boo and Beeker started saying really strange things from their desks.

While reading her chat-box, Boo said, "He's making more than us now." "I know . . . His girlfriend is on his side," Beeker replied. "Hospital work is so easy," Boo went on, "We know all about her." And then Beeker said, "He thinks he's smart."

Wow, I thought to myself! They're doing it again. This is definitely another NSA employment set-up. How did Beeker and Boo know I just got a raise from Herbert upstairs, a few minutes ago? How did they know Jennifer was working at a hospital now? How did they even know I had a girlfriend, since I'd just met them the day before?

I shook my head. They were spying on me in real-time and it made me angry. I looked around the ceiling and walls for surveillance cameras. There were none! We were working inside a two-story high factory building with steel and metal walls. There were no hidden cameras in the building and I was sure of it. How were they spying on me in real-time, I wondered?

I thought of quitting right there and then. I took a break and called Jennifer and told her what was going on. She reminded me that my student loan payments were due, and that I should keep working there until I find another job. She said to just ignore them.

When I came back from break, Beeker said, "The Company likes you and doesn't want to lose you." "They just want to put you in a box, like the rest of us," he said. "OK, whatever," I replied. "We've got X-Ray machines to test, so let's get back to work," Beeker said.

That night I had another long talk with Jennifer. I explained everything to her about the spying in real-time. She said she believed every word I told her. "That's really creepy," she said. "Do you think our phones are tapped?" she asked. "Yes, absolutely," I answered. She thought about it and became angry. "That's illegal to tap phones without a warrant," she said. "That's illegal and Un-Constitutional."

"They're the NSA and they don't care," I told her. "These people are psychos and they're spying on you and me in real-time," I said. "They keep setting up fake jobs for me, when I've told them I don't want to work for them." She suddenly looked distressed and closed all the blinds and curtains in our apartment.

The next day at work, I looked at Beeker and Boo sitting behind their desks. I decided to hurt Beeker and punch him in the face. Just another Navy goon, I thought to myself. Then they started doing it again -- The spying-talk on the chat-box.

"Warrants are so old-fashioned," Boo said just as I sat down to work. "Did you pay your taxes on time?" Beeker said back to her. "I don't want Uncle Sam after me," he went on. "Just do as you're told," Boo said next. "And don't ask questions," Beeker followed-up her words.

I got up out of my chair and walked over to Beeker. I clenched my fist and almost punched him in the face. "Is that your real name . . . Beeker?" I asked him calmly. "I was a nerd in high school, until I joined the Navy," he said in his whiny voice. "They called me Beeker in high school," he said.

I noticed he also had a chat-box on his computer. They were both reading out loud from chat-boxes. These NSA people are psychos, I thought to myself. I punched my own fist in front of Beeker and went back to work, thinking of hurting him.

That afternoon, Herbert brought down another technician he just hired. He said his name was Billy, and he would have a desk next to mine. Billy looked like a hippy, with really long hair, and an AC/DC shirt on. He was about 6-foot-2, with arms like like a boxer. I noticed he had a tattoo on his arm that said *Semper Fi*.

Beeker showed Billy the same X-Ray machine testing and procedures he showed me. Beeker said they were ramping-up production because we just got a new factory order for these machines. He said we could start working overtime next week if we wanted to.

Billy didn't talk much and he acted normal like me. I asked him about the *Semper Fi* tattoo? He said he was a US Marine veteran of the Iraq War. I noticed Billy was quiet and calm like me, unlike Beeker and Boo.

I told Billy about the Navy goons we were working with. "Navy goons?" Billy laughed out loud. "Yeah," I said. "I don't like Navy people and never did," Billy replied. "They make me want to puke . . . Like I'm on a ship or something."

Billy looked at Beeker and Boo. "I hate Navy people," Billy snarled at them. "I have really bad memories of them from Iraq," he said. So, now it was two against two. It was me and Billy against the Navy goons.

Chapter 6 - X-Ray Attack

No nation can preserve its freedom in the midst of continual warfare. -James Madison

People who live in glass houses shouldn't. -Foggy (NSA spook)

******

The next day at work went easy for about an hour or so. Beeker and Boo both stopped the spying-talk on the chat-box until around 10:00 AM. Then they started it up again, while I was working quietly at my desk. Out of nowhere, they started saying really strange things again.

"Uncle Sam is watching you," Beeker said first. "He pays his taxes on time," Boo said back. "She hid a sex toy in the third drawer down . . . It's next to the bed," Beeker said next. "It's not that big," Boo said back to Beeker.

Wow, I thought to myself! Did I just hear that? My girlfriend has a sex toy hidden next to our bed? I didn't know that . . . How did Beeker and Boo know that? How could they see into the drawers next to our bed? How can they spy on me and Jennifer in our bedroom?

Just then, Billy showed up for work, two hours late. He looked like he had a hang-over or something. "Aww . . . My head," he said. He powered-up the test machine. "What are these Danger! Warning! Caution! stickers?" Billy asked me. "Beeker says he's a Navy Radar Technician," I told him. "He says we just have to follow procedures," I explained.

"These machines are dangerous," Billy replied. "I know," I said, "I almost quit on my first day." "I didn't get hired here to work on dangerous radiation equipment . . . They didn't tell me that in the job description," Billy said.

"Welcome to The Company," I laughed at him. "It's me and you against them," I told Billy. "Me and you?" Billy asked. "Yeah," I said, "Beeker and Boo are NSA goons." "They're spying on us at work right now," I told him. "What?" Billy asked. "It's a long story," I said.

After lunch, Beeker said he had a new project for me. He led me to the X-Ray chamber near the 12 VDC battery testing area. "We need you to test out this new device," Beeker told me. "It won't take long, just a few minutes," he said.

"OK," I said and he led me into the X-Ray chamber. There were huge "Danger! Warning! Caution!" signs all over the chamber. Beeker showed me a circuit to test with an oscilloscope, and gave me the schematics to use. "Don't worry," Beeker said, "It's just a test." "Take your time and follow the procedures," he told me.

I heard a humming-noise as the X-Ray chamber ramped-up. Beeker then slammed the door shut and locked it! Out of nowhere, Billy ran up to Beeker and punched him in the face! Billy unlocked the door and shouted, "Get out of there!" "Beeker just tried to kill you!" "He tried to kill you with X-Rays!"

"I know," I said catching my breath, "Beeker is an NSA goon!" Beeker was lying on the floor with a broken nose and blood all over the place. I round-housed him a few times on the floor. Billy gave him a few good kicks, for good measure.

"That's crazy!" Billy looked at me. "I know," I said, "The NSA is after me and my girlfriend." "What for?" Billy asked. "Because I refuse to work for them . . . Because I told them to fuck off about twenty times," I told him. "The NSA, huh?" Billy asked. "Yes, sir, the real NSA -- The goons from Fort Meade," I explained.

"I'm going upstairs right now and quitting this job," I told him. Billy thought about it. "Tell you what . . . Meet me after work at the Wild West bar down the road," he said. "I want to hear the full story." "OK," I said, "I know that bar, and I'll see you around 7:00 PM with my girlfriend."

I went upstairs and found the Navy goon Herbert in his cubicle. I told him how Beeker just tried to kill me with X-Rays. "What?" Herbert said, "I know nothing, nothing!" I grabbed his Navy football and smacked him in the face a few times. "You're lucky I don't really hurt you," I told him. I walked out of the factory, thinking about how I was being spied upon in real-time.

I called Jennifer and told her what had happened. "Get out of there!" Jennifer yelled, "Call the police on them!" She started crying on the phone. "Call the police on them!" she cried again. "I don't know . . . It's no big deal," I told her.

"It's just another NSA employment set-up . . . These people are psychos, and they won't leave me alone." "They just tried to kill you!" she shouted over the phone. "The NSA is evil!" I told her, "They're spying on you and me!"

Around 7:00 PM, I met Billy at the Wild West bar. I was going to bring Jennifer along, but thought better of it. Billy asked where my girlfriend was? "I left her at home," I said. "Beeker tried to kill you with X-Rays," he said. "Yeah, I know," I said, "This has been going on for years . . . Beeker and Boo work for the NSA."

"The NSA?" he asked seriously. "Yeah, the NSA," I replied. "How do you know that?" he looked me in the eyes. "Because I know," I said. Billy shook his head for a moment and laughed.

"After what happened today at work, I believe you," he said. Billy ordered a Kentucky whiskey and took a shot. "I didn't take fire in Iraq for this bullshit," he said. "Those fuckers in command are idiots."

"They're spying on every American in America in real-time," I told him. "They found me camping out in the forest and then tried to kill me with a psycho from Florida," I explained. "I thought they had some sort of tracking device on my Jeep, but they didn't."

Billy was listening carefully. "Did you have your cell phone with you or even turned off?" he asked. "No, I didn't have a cell phone with me because I'm not stupid," I answered. "I have degree in Telecommunications Electronics," I told him.

"They can track your cell phone even when it's turned off," I told him. "You can take the battery out and there's still a capacitor inside they can activate remotely," I said. "I know that," Billy nodded his head at me, "It's called electronics."

"Years ago, they broke into my house and left the door-handles hanging -- As a joke," I told him. "It's not the FBI . . . It's the NSA and CIA." "I called the local Sheriff and he came out and told me it was spooks," I went on. "They didn't steal a thing, they just broke in for nothing." I looked around the bar and made sure no one was listening to us. "The fuckers are spying on me and my girlfriend," I told him.

Billy looked distressed. I ordered a Kentucky whiskey for my new friend. Billy took another shot and became angry. "I believe you," he said. "You wouldn't believe what I saw in Iraq." "This country is so fucked-up it's not even funny," he became angry. "The politicians have ruined America and there's nothing left worth saving!" Billy said loudly.

He looked around the bar and then quieted down. "Hey, we can't really talk here at this bar," he said. "Follow me over to my place . . . I've got some tequila and whiskey at home." "Do you have beer as a chaser?" I asked. "Yeah, I've got two cases of beer," he said. "OK," I said, "I'll follow you over to your place."

I followed Billy over to his apartment, not far from the bar down the road. He had a huge *Semper Fi* banner hanging on the wall above two crossed rifles. He had two M-1 Garand's with his Marine Corps. hat in the center above the rifles. His apartment was a mess, with beer cans and Playboy magazines lying around.

He saw me looking at his *Semper Fi* rifles. "Very cool," I said. "The words *Semper Fi* are burned into my brain," he told me. "You wouldn't believe what I went through in Iraq." "I saw house-to-house combat, and my buddy got his head blown-off with an RPG."

"That's bad," I shook my head. "I knew a teacher who went through the Vietnam War," I told him. "He said the same thing -- How his buddy got his head blown-off with a rocket in Vietnam."

Billy got some beers out of the fridge and brought over a bottle of tequila. "Yeah, I've always hated Navy people," he said. "They're the scum of the military." "They hide out at sea on ships, while people like me get shot at in house-to-house combat."

He was serious about it and was angry. He showed me his medals from the Iraq War. "OK," I said, "I've known lots of dudes in the Army and Air Force, and they're my old friends."

Billy interrupted me, "You have no idea about the kind of bullshit I saw in Iraq!" "We conquered the fucking beach, and President Roths backed-off . . . Like a coward!"

"This country is so fucked-up!" I said. "Fucked-up!" Billy shouted. "This country is fucked-up beyond the stone age!" He offered me another beer and a shot of tequila. "I know," I said and took another shot of tequila.

"They're spying on me and my girlfriend," I told him. "How?" Billy asked, "How are they spying on you and your girlfriend?" "It's in real-time and without any video cameras or even cell phone cameras," I explained. "Yeah?" Billy asked. "I'm absolutely sure of it," I said.

"Tell me more?" Billy asked. "It all started years ago, when I met the NSA and CIA," I told him. "Over and over, they were somehow spying on me in real-time everywhere I went," I explained.

"They knew where I was, working at my old job inside a factory . . . Eating pizza at the same place every day," I explained. "It has nothing to do with cell phone tracking, cell tower triangulation, or cell phone spying -- None of it," I told Billy.

Billy took another shot of tequila. He became quiet and thought about it. Finally, his eyes lit up. "Satellites," he said, "They're spying on you in real-time with satellites." "That's it!" I said, "It's the only logical conclusion." "I've thought of that for years," I told him.

"Hell," Billy said, "You wouldn't believe what I saw in Iraq." "My boss had a laptop with real-time satellite surveillance of the battlefield." "It wasn't drones or spy planes flying above -- It was satellites that can see through buildings," he smiled at me.

"No way," I said, "That's it!" "Yeah," he said, "They can see through buildings in real-time, even into the ground looking for munitions." "How do you think we won the Iraq War?" he laughed. "We had fucking satellites targeting every weapon they had buried underground."

I turned up the AC/DC on the stereo. "Give me another shot," I said. "Yes, sir," Billy answered. "If you're right, and I believe you -- They can see crystal clear into this apartment," he said. "They can read the cover-month of that Playboy on the table," he said.

Billy became quiet and serious for a moment. "So, you met the NSA and CIA?" he asked. "Yeah, it's a long story," I told him. "Tell me about it?" Billy asked me. "Those guys are the elites . . . I'm just another Marine from Camp Pendleton."

"No," I told him. "You Marines conquered Iwo Jima and won D-Day . . . You set all of us all free." "You Marines are the *Real Americans*, not a bunch of Navy goons spying on people with satellites," I went on.

He thought about it and became angry. "That's totally illegal," he said. "That's a total violation of the Constitution and Bill of Rights!" "Yeah," I said, "The Deep State in Washington, DC has turned against the American people."

"That's fucking treason!" Billy shouted, "Turning military satellites on Americans in America!" "They did it," I said. "They're spying on us right now in your apartment."

Billy looked up at the ceiling and flipped them off. "Fuck you traitors!" he shouted at them. "I didn't take fire in Iraq for this bullshit back here at home," he said. "I swore an Oath to the Constitution and Bill of Rights!"

Chapter 7 - Invasion of Privacy

Republics and Democracies have lost their liberties by way of passing from civilian to quasi-military status. -Douglas MacArthur

We're on a fishing expedition for Americans. -Captain Kurtz (NSA Spook)

*****

The next day after Jennifer went to work, I looked into the third drawer next to our bed. Sure enough, Jennifer had a sex toy hidden under her clothes. How did Beeker and Boo know that? I looked up at the ceiling of our bedroom and I knew it! They were spying on me and Jennifer in our bedroom with satellites! I was absolutely sure of it.

I went to the Desert University library and started researching spy satellites. I spent the day searching college-level databases and books for any information I could find. I quickly discovered there weren't any real books on spy satellites since 1984. All I could find were worthless old 1960's Cold War textbooks from the JFK-era.

I decided to use the scientific method, as I was taught in college, and figure out these spy satellites. Using deduction, induction, and even the human logic of Philosophy -- I figured it all out. It was a fact that the NSA and CIA were spying on me in real-time since 1999, when I first met Clint Franco. It was only logical that they were using spy satellites to do it. There is no other logical explanation for the "see inside of buildings" technology I'd been exposed to.

I started reading the books I'd found. Modern spy satellites see through buildings in real time -- Even through parking garages. They transmit data to collection points around the planet using satellite uplink/downlink dishes. Since the data is digital, it's stored forever at NSA/CIA data centers for later analysis. The implications of this are incredible, to say the least.

I started searching the Internet for more information, since I couldn't find any technical satellite books past 1984. I came across 1990's business information on billion-dollar satellite companies building constellations of satellites. Several of these companies failed due to financing problems in the early 1990's.

But, then I discovered Globalcore. They were a billion-dollar company financed by a South American government. In 1990, the US government launched Project 66/6 for Globalcore. The government launched 72 satellites (66 + 6) into space for them. The planet Earth was encircled by a grid of 66 Low Earth Orbit (LEO) satellites (with 6 spares as backup). Project 66/6 went off without a single hitch. Not one rocket blew-up, and the satellite grid was operational around 1994. It was sold to the public as a commercial, not military, satellite grid encircling the planet.

Globalcore marketed this as a satellite telephone system for airlines, pilots, and ships at sea. The Globalcore satellite telephone system worked anywhere on the planet, at any altitude, and in any weather. The Globalcore unit can make phone calls, send text messages, and provide Internet service 24/7.

It also allows real-time tracking of the unit anywhere on Earth: At the South Pole, or North Pole, or on a ship at sea. Or even flying 40,000 feet high in a jet airplane. That's it, I thought. Project 66/6 was a global spy satellite grid, built by the US government.

That night I told Jennifer about it, and showed her all the books and information I found at the library. "That's incredible!" she said, "I've always known you're really smart." She kissed me and said, "You figured it all out . . . I think you're a genius." "Yeah, babe," I said, "They're spying on all of us with NSA satellites."

"Are they spying on us in our apartment right now with satellites?" she became serious. "Yes, then can see us right now," I answered. "They can see us, hear us, and can zoom-in to our papers, magazines, and sex toys," I told her.

"Our sex toys?" she looked surprised. She thought about it and then became angry. "How did you know that?" she asked me, "How did you know about my sex toy?" "The NSA told me a sex toy was hidden next to our bed," I answered.

"That's evil!" she shouted, "That's a total invasion of privacy!" "I know," I said and looked her in the eyes. "They're spying on our bedroom with military satellites," I explained. "They can see through buildings and parking garages." Jennifer started crying. "That's horrible! That's illegal!" she shouted. "That's not American!"

"No, it's not," I said. "We have some very evil people in the government right now." "Evil people? That's beyond evil!" she said. "There's Nazis inside the government right now," I told her, "They're inside the NSA." She looked at me and started crying again.

"Human privacy is a need like oxygen," she said, "It's not something you want." "It's too late now," I told her. Jennifer became really quiet for a minute, wiping away her tears. "There's a reason people have sex in the dark . . . Because it's human," she said finally. "I know, babe," I hugged her. "Privacy is a basic human need," she said, "It's something human."

I kissed Jennifer, "It's all right," I said. "They're evil!" She was crying again in my arms. "It's OK," I said. "America is bigger than a bunch of NSA goons hiding in the shadows of Washington, DC." "The Founding Father's told us what to do when tyranny returns to America."

I called up Billy and told him I wanted to talk to him. "Yeah, dude, come on over," he said. "I just bought a bottle of Kentucky whiskey." "Do you have any beers left?" I asked. "Yeah, just enough for both of us," he laughed. "OK, I'll be right over," I said.

Billy looked half-drunk when I met him at his apartment. "What's up?" he asked. "Not much, except some serious spying by the NSA," I replied. "You want a beer and a shot?" he asked. "Yeah," I said, "I could use a shot right now." Billy gave me a beer and a shot of whiskey. I slammed the beer and took a shot. "You wouldn't believe what I found out at the library today," I told him.

"The library?" Billy asked. "Yeah, I did some research," I said, "The fuckers are spying on America with military satellites." "There's a grid of 66 spy satellites circled around the planet," I told him. Billy shook his head and thought about it. "I believe it," he said, "I told you what I saw in Iraq . . . With that spy satellite computer my boss had." "It blew my mind, seeing what spy satellites can do in real-time," he went on.

"They can see into buildings in real-time?" I asked him. "They can see every fucking detail inside a building in real-time," he answered. "They can watch you fuck your girlfriend in your bedroom if they want to," he explained. "They can zoom-in and focus on that Playboy magazine . . . They can read the cover," he said. "What's worse is -- It's all digital data, which means it's stored forever on a computer." "I know," I said, "That's what I found out today at the library."

"They're doing it right now," I told him. "That's treason," Billy said back. "The Constitution and Bill of Rights are very clear," he said. "The NSA has no authority to spy on Americans in America." He took another shot of whiskey. "Those military satellites were built to spy on foreign enemies, not domestic affairs." Billy became quiet and angry. "Fuck!" he shouted, "Those spy satellites were built to win the Cold War against Russia, not watch you fuck your girlfriend in your apartment."

"I've read the Constitution and Bill of Rights from start to finish," I told him. "We had to read it in a college class I took," I said. "The Bill of Rights are very clear and it's meant to be taken literally, like the Founding Father's intended."

"The government is fucked beyond repair!" Billy shouted out loud. He took another shot. "I didn't watch my buddy get his head blown off with a rocket for this bullshit!" "I didn't serve in Iraq for this Commie-Fascist bullshit!" he shouted.

"That's really bad," I said. "Yeah," Billy replied, "My buddy got his head blown off with a rocket." He became calm and quiet. "I joined the Marines because I thought I was fighting for freedom, liberty, and democracy," he said drunkenly. "I swore an Oath to the Constitution, and now it looks like we've got a bunch of traitors inside the government."

Billy became very serious and angry. "Those military satellites were never intended to be turned against the American people," he said, "That's fucking treason!" "Yeah, it's treason -- Straight up treason by the NSA," I replied. "What can we do about it?" I asked him. "I don't know . . . Build an Old West gallows in Washington, DC and hang the bastards?" Billy answered. "Maybe give them a fair trial and shoot them with a Marine firing squad?"

"I don't know about that? That's kinda crazy?" I looked at him and laughed. "Do you realize the implications of the government spying on Americans with satellites?" I asked him. "They could declare Martial Law for any reason, and start rounding-up Americans they don't like," I said. "It's the oldest story in history . . . The return of tyranny and totalitarianism."

"The Founding Father's warned us that tyranny would return to America," Billy replied. "Thomas Jefferson warned future generations of Americans about the blood of patriots and tyrants."

I took another shot and stared at the Semper Fi banner and the M-1 Garand's on the wall. Billy saw me looking at the Semper Fi banner and his World War II rifles. He looked at me and took another shot, "I know how to solve problems . . . I'm a Marine."

He went into the other room and came back out with a brand new AR-10 rifle. "It's a .308 Winchester," he said, "Check out the night vision scope I got when I left the service." "Nice," I said. "This fucker is Marine Corps. approved," he laughed. "It's got a laser beam sight!"

"I've got an AR-15, but it's just good for coyotes," I told him. "I almost went to Marine Corps. sniper school," Billy told me, "But they put me on the .50 caliber instead." "The .50?" I asked him. "Yes, sir, the .50," he said. "Fully automatic, Yes, sir!" "US Marines!" Billy shouted out of nowhere.

He took another shot of whiskey and stared at his Semper Fi banner. I slammed another beer and took a shot. "I've got an idea," I said. "These spy satellites are spying upon Americans right?" "Yes, sir," Billy answered. "Why don't we pull the plug on it?" I asked him. "Why don't we pull the plug on the satellite computers?"

"Yeah, we could do that," Billy answered. "We could pull the plug on the satellites and the NSA computers storing all the data." "The satellite grid circling the planet transmits data back and forth to the NSA uplink/downlink satellite dishes," I told him. "All we have to do is pull the plug on the uplink/downlink dishes."

"Yes, sir," Billy said. "The satellite grid is just like any other computer -- Pull the plug on it!" "Those big white domes you see at NSA bases are the uplink/downlink stations," I told him. "I saw that in a satellite book today."

"You're right," Billy said after thinking about it. "The whole satellite grid is just a big computer, and we just have to pull the plug on it." Billy took another shot and was wasted-drunk at this point.

"We could cut the power lines to the uplink/downlink

stations," he said. "Those satellite uplink/downlink dishes use a lot of power," he said drunkenly. "We just have to pull the plug on the satellite dishes."

Billy was wasted-drunk, and I was also. It was getting late and I thought of Jennifer waiting for me at home. "It's 1776 again and you Marines are gonna win it!" "Yes, sir," Billy said back. "The Marines will defend freedom and liberty at any cost."

I went home to Jennifer and she was crying. "I'm scared," she said, "They're spying on us." "They're spying on us in our own house and bedroom." I hugged and kissed her and said, "It doesn't matter now . . . We've got the Marines on our side." "It's OK," I told her, "They have no idea what's coming for them."

"This is America! This is the Land of the Free and the Home of the Brave!" I said drunkenly. Jennifer looked at me and stopped crying. "The Marines are on our side?" she asked. "Yes, they are," I told her. "They have no idea what's coming for them!" I told her again.

Chapter 8 - New Stasi America

I repeat once again: We must know everything! Nothing can get past us! -Erich Mielke

You have nothing to fear, if you have nothing to hide.
-Joseph Goebbels

*****

The next day Billy called me up right after high noon. "I have to talk to you," he said. "Come over to my place . . . It's important," he told me. "OK," I said, "I'll be there in about an hour." "No, come over here right now," he said, "It's important." "OK," I said, "I'm on the way."

I drove over right away and Billy let me in his apartment, and locked the door quickly after I was in. He was sober and looked wired on coffee. "What's up?" I asked him. "The fuckers started talking shit to me today at work," he said. "Beeker and Boo are spying on me."

"Yeah," I said, "I believe it . . . I told you so." "The fuckers started saying all this crazy shit to me . . . About my DUI from four years ago," he was angry. He shook his head. "I tried to pick-up a fat-chick at the bar the other night, and they were laughing at me about it," he said. "How did they know I tried to pick-up a fat-chick at the bar?"

"Were they reading the chat-boxes on their computers?" I asked him. "Yeah," he said, "They were." "That's what they did to me," I told him. "I told you they're NSA goons . . . They're spying on all of us with satellites." Billy became crazy-angry. "I punched Beeker in the head again and almost hit Boo," he said.

"Right on," I said, "They're traitors -- All of them!" "Fucking traitors in the NSA!" Billy agreed with me. "I'm just a Marine and I don't know nothing about it." "No," I said to him, "You don't know about it." I looked at him very seriously. "It's all Deep State stuff . . . This stuff is not on the Fascist TV-news for old people."

"Fascist?" Billy asked. "I don't know," I said, "There's Nazis inside the US government," I told him. "I'm sure of it . . . There's Nazis inside the NSA and they're spying on every man, woman, and child in America."

45

Billy became quiet for a minute and stared at his Semper Fi banner. "I believe it," he said finally. He looked at his M-1 Garand rifles on the wall. "I'm a Marine sworn to uphold and defend the Constitution of the United States," he said. "I will not relent . . . To uphold freedom and liberty for all Americans." "Yes, sir!" I said to Billy. "It's my duty to kill tyrants foreign and domestic," he said.

"You Marines are the ones who conquered Iwo Jima and won D-Day, Korea, and Vietnam," I told him. "You Marines conquered Iwo Jima a thousand times." "Yes, sir," Billy answered. He was staring at his rifles on the wall. "The Marines conquered Iwo Jima like George Washington conquered the British Navy," I told him.

"What's strange is how the new guy they hired to fill your job was from Germany," Billy said. "He said his name was Dieter, and he had a German accent." "That's the NSA," I told him, "That's who they are." He raised his eyebrows.

"Did you notice the greased-back Hitler haircut Herbert has? All he needs is the Hitler mustache?" I asked him. "I did," Billy answered and looked alarmed. "There's goddamned Nazis inside the NSA," I told him.

"That's fucking crazy . . . And I know what you're talking about," he agreed. Billy looked at his Semper Fi banner again. He thought about it. "I know what you mean," he said, "I see it now . . . I get it."

"I did more research at the library today, and did some thinking," I told him. "You know they've turned US military satellites upon Americans in America?" I asked Billy. "Yeah," Billy answered.

"You know those satellites see everything and it's stored forever in NSA databases . . . Guess what that means?" I asked him. "I don't know?" he looked at me.

"It means the fuckers can watch a bank robbery four years ago in the middle of New York City or Los Angeles on a NSA computer," I told him. "They can type in any date, time, or place into a NSA computer and zoom-in on anything that was recorded by the spy satellites."

"Hell, yeah," Billy said. "Yeah, think about it," I told him, "Our lives are being recorded in real-time by NSA spy satellites." "That's treason!" Billy shouted. "Those satellites were meant to spy on Russians not Americans!"

"It's a fact that people inside the government made this happen," I replied. "They're not *Real Americans* like you or me." "It's possible the government has set-up thousands of court proceedings using NSA satellites." "They can set-up anyone in America and keep it a secret in courtrooms." "Even your own lawyer doesn't know what's going on."

"That's fucking treason to turn military satellites upon America!" Billy was crazy-angry. He took one of his M-1 Garand's off the wall. He chambered it like a Marine. "That's fucking treason against the American people!" he shouted.

Billy started pacing around his apartment with his M-1 Garand. He looked out the blinds of his apartment windows. "It's time to solve some problems," he said. "They taught me how to solve problems in the Marines."

"Yes, sir," I answered. "The people who turned the satellites on America are not *Real Americans* -- They're traitors." "It's possible that your girlfriend in jail was set-up by NSA secret evidence in court," I told him.

In the library, I found a book on how to keep secret evidence out of court rooms. It was written by the Intelligence Community for the Safety Police of America (SPA).

The book describes what they call Spying Streets (SS) across America, using military-intelligence people inside local city police departments. The book describes how to go around the Constitution in courtrooms to protect what they call sources and methods.

"Holy Fuck!" Billy shouted. "That's like the Soviet Union or Nazi Germany," he said. "I also found books on the old East German Stasi," I told him. "They would put hidden cameras into people's bedrooms and then try to control them with what they saw . . . Sound familiar?" I asked him.

"Sounds like Beeker and Boo," Billy answered. "They would tell them how they were spying on them," I explained. "That's the important part . . . How they talk to the people being spied upon." "The NSA is playing Stasi games with their satellites turned upon America."

47

"OK," Billy said, "So what are we gonna do about it?" "What are we gonna do about the NSA spy satellites?" "I don't know," I answered. "The Founding Father's told us that tyranny would return to America in the future." "The Founding Father's warned us about the blood of patriots and tyrants."

"Let's pull the plug on the satellite computer in the sky," Billy said. "The spy satellite grid depends upon those uplink/downlink stations to work." "Those big white satellite domes are the main-line plugs to the system." "It's all just a big computer that can be shut-down."

"Yeah," I replied, "Sounds about right . . . Sounds like a job for the patriotic Marines of America." "Yes, sir," Billy answered. "I've got an idea," he went on, "What if me and my Marine buddies start a new Continental Army, just like George Washington did against the British spies of 1776?"

"What if me and my Marine buddies start a *Real American* patriot army to shut-down the NSA spy satellites?" "Sounds good to me," I answered. "Semper Fi," I said to Billy. Billy laughed, "Hey, let's go to the Cabaret Club and check out the dancers."

"Yeah, I could use a drink," I said. "I think the nude room opens at 3:00 PM," I laughed, "100% naked fine pussy!" Billy laughed at me, "Let's go!"

Chapter 9 - John the Ghost

Our way of life is under attack. Those who make themselves our enemy are advancing around the globe. -John F. Kennedy

All that is necessary for the triumph of evil is that good men do nothing. -Edmund Burke

*****

I followed Billy to the Cabaret Club in my Jeep. When we got there we found out the nude room didn't open until 5:00 PM, so we started drinking at the bar. After about an hour of drinking, an old man in a black trench-coat came in the door and sat next to us. He started doing shots of whiskey with beer chasers.

Billy kept talking about the NSA and how he punched Beeker in the face again. It slowly became obvious the old man in the trench-coat was listening to us at the bar. It made me angry, because I knew he was a spook. The NSA called him up on his cell phone to spy on me and Billy at the Cabaret Club.

Billy started getting drunk and talking to him. I told Billy he was a spook and to shut-up about it. "Let's go check out the dancers on the stage," I distracted him. "No, wait," the old man said suddenly. "I have some information you guys might want to hear." "I'm on your side . . . I'm not the enemy."

"Yeah, old man?" Billy looked at him, "I bet you are." "I'll buy you guys a round if you'll just listen to me," he told Billy with his Boston accent. "OK," Billy said, "Let's go sit near the dancers on the stage."

The old man nodded and introduced himself. "I'm John from Boston," he explained. "I've worked in the government for a long time . . . Many, many years." His eyes lit up like a ghost or something.

"I heard your talk about the NSA and the spying going on," he said. "You're absolutely right about the treason of the people in Washington, DC." "I've been in and out of government for 50 years." He spoke quietly with a heavy Boston accent. "So . . . What's the info old man?" Billy asked him.

Just then, a blonde stripper put her boobies in my face, and was smiling at me. "You are hot," I told her. She laughed and showed me more. "What's your name?" she asked me. "Johnny," I said. "I like you Johnny," she winked at me. I put a dollar bill in her panties and she smiled again. "What's your name?" I asked her. "Daisy," she smiled.

"Like I said . . . I was deep inside the government for 50 years, until I retired," John explained. "I saw it all -- The wars and murders . . . And assassinations." "I remember when Hitler was on the front page of the newspaper." "You're that old?" Billy asked him.

John's eyes grew dark. "I was born in 1937 and I still remember it all," he answered slowly. "America was a free country until when they killed President Kennedy . . . And his brother Bobby." "That's when it all changed," he said. "Some serious dark forces took over Washington, DC back then." "I know because I was in those meetings," he told us.

"I'm retired Navy and I saw it all." He paused and thought about it. "It was hot back then in the Cold War days . . . Very hot." "You guys are so young, and you don't have a clue about what happened back then."

"So, what's the info old man?" Billy asked him again. John ordered a round of drinks and took a shot of whiskey. Daisy kept putting her boobies in my face and I smiled at her.

"Are you going to be in the nude room?" I asked her. "No," she said, "I'm just a dancer." "Too bad," I laughed and put $10 in her panties. She winked at me again. "What do you want?" I asked her.

"Very few people know this, but around 1990 President Roth secretly turned all of the resources of the NSA and CIA onto the American people," he said. John's face became very serious. "That means the NSA, CIA, NRO, NGA -- All of it."

"NGA? What's that?" Billy asked. "National Geo-Spatial Intelligence Agency," John replied. "President Roth turned half of our spy satellites from Russia onto the USA for domestic surveillance."

"That's illegal and goes against the Constitution and Bill of Rights," I said to John. John nodded and agreed, "Yes, it's illegal and Un-American at best." "But it was all done secretly with declarations of National Security." John took another shot of whiskey. His eyes rolled in his head.

"Of course, President Roth had connections to Nazi bankers from World War II," he went on. "He was a US Navy man turned treacherous Nazi back in the 1950's."

John paused and thought about it. "It's the story of our time," he said. "President Roth wasn't alone and many military men inside the government became Nazis," he explained. "There's something about the NSA that breeds traitors."

He shook his head thinking about it. "They're military men with a lust for power and control." "They hate liberty and freedom . . . And they're control-freaks."

"They hate liberty and freedom?" Billy asked, "What the fuck did I fight for in Iraq?" "I'm a goddamned Marine!" John looked at Billy coldly and then stared at him. He took another shot of whiskey and suddenly became angry. "They're all cheats and liars!" he said loudly.

"Around 2000, the NSA was taken over by a gang of vicious traitors . . . I sat in meetings with them over and over." John shook his head again. "They all had one thing in common . . . They were GTANK Corporation members since the 1990's." "I was a GTANK Corporation member, and I was in the same meetings with them."

"Since the 1990's the GTANK Corporation has been indoctrinating American politicians, media, police, and military men to build a globalist New World Order," John explained.

"That's fucking crazy!" I interrupted him, "I read that in my college textbooks." "About how the UN was infiltrated by the Soviet Union in the 1950's . . . To build a globalist government." "Their goal was to destroy American freedom and democracy," I told him.

Billy took a drink and started slamming shots. "OK, old man," he said to John, "I believe you and tell us more." John stared at him coldly and took another shot of whiskey. His eyes rolled again in his head. "Like I said, around 2000, a gang of vicious traitors took over the NSA."

Just then, Daisy came back up to me on the stage and put her flashing LED high-heels in the air. She had LED lights in her high-heels. "Hey, Johnny," she said to me, "Do you like to party?" "Yeah, Daisy," I smiled at her, "And I like your high-heels."

John became distracted and was staring at Daisy. "Give me another shot," he said drunkenly. We were all getting drunk really fast, waiting for the nude room to open. "How long until the nude room opens?" I asked Billy. "Not long," he said, "Listen to John . . . He's telling us the truth about the NSA."

John's face changed. "I am telling you the truth," he said to Billy. "Yes, sir," Billy said to John. "Goddamned treason has been going on since 1990!" he told Billy. "President Roth and his generals secretly turned America into a NSA spy satellite grid, and you can forget about the Constitution and Bill of Rights."

"No!" I said to him. "That's bullshit . . . We, the People, can easily restore our rights, freedoms, and privacy." "It's easy . . . We can shut-down the NSA spy satellites turned upon America."

John looked at me coldly. "Admiral Bayer, Admiral Ziegler, and General Haas all conspired against the Constitution and Bill of Rights," he said. "I sat in the fucking meetings!" he snarled.

"Right before my eyes, they hired twenty NSA lawyers to find a thousand ways around the Fourth Amendment and Supreme Court privacy rulings."

"They illegally subverted the Constitution and Bill of Rights with NSA lawyers." "They held secret meetings at the NSA figuring out how to dismantle the Bill of Rights." "I told my boss at the Pentagon what they were doing, and he told me to shut-up about it."

"OK, old man," Billy said, "I've heard enough and I believe you." Billy stared at his drink. "You don't get it!" John snarled at Billy. "We're talking about a gang of traitors and lawyers inside the NSA who destroyed the Constitution with paperwork and secret laws."

"They've got illegal dossiers on millions of Americans without a warrant, and they're using US military spy satellites to do it." "They're building a totalitarian NSA database on American citizens, and it's a turn-key system."

John looked Billy in the eyes. "The Deep State was born when a gang of traitors inside the CIA killed President Kennedy and took secret power like a military junta," John told him.

Billy grinned at him and lit up a cigar. "I've got some

buddies in the Marines," he said. "We swore an Oath to uphold the Constitution and Bill of Rights." John shook his head sadly. "Rest assured, old man, the Marines are on duty," he told John. "The Constitution and Bill of Rights are bigger than a gang of NSA traitors and lawyers."

Billy looked at John seriously, "We believe in 1776, not the bullshit of today." "We believe in a higher calling like George Washington and Thomas Jefferson." "We also believe in a higher power called God." "America is a free country and shall remain free, like 1776 or 2076!"

John's eyes lit up and he grinned at Billy. "What else can you tell us about the NSA?" Billy asked John. "Around 2005, Admiral Xiaboa joined our meetings," he answered. "He said they were concerned because they couldn't control the Free and Open Internet."

"He said the NSA had plans to militarize the Internet, so they can control it all and spy on the entire planet." John took another drink and thought about it. "They hate the Free and Open Internet because they can't control it."

"Admiral Xiaboa is a psychotic and sociopath, with connections to Chinese computer companies," he went on. "He gave us a presentation on NSA plans to militarize the Internet and turn it into a global NSA spy machine."

"Admiral Xiaboa?" Billy asked, "I've seen him on TV." "That's right," John nodded. "He's really good at lying to Congress on TV." "He joked to me once about how he controls members of Congress on the intelligence committees."

"He controls members of Congress?" Billy raised his eyebrows. "It's all dirty tricks and NSA spying," John replied. "Do you know how easy it is to spy on Americans with military satellites?" Billy stared at his drink, thinking about it.

"Of course, the NSA and Chinese have the same goal of total surveillance of the population -- Communist or American." "It's all about government control of the population," John went on.

"Do you know what an Electrical Engineer can do with the hardware of a Chinese cell phone?" John asked. "I do," I answered John. "I know how to engineer hardware and software -- Bits and bytes."

"I can engineer a cell phone to be the ultimate spy device of a globalist New World Order," I told him. "I can program 200 secret backdoors and phone-homes into a cell phone to *spy on everyone*."

John stared at Billy and became angry again. "The NSA is evil and should be shut-down immediately by the President or Congress." "The NSA must be shut-down for the good of every man, woman, and child in America!"

"Tell us more," Billy said. "Allen Dulles, the founder of the CIA was fired by President Kennedy. About two years later, JFK was assassinated in a coup d'etat in Dallas. That's when the military took over the civilian US government."

Just then, Daisy appeared again on the stage. She leaned down and almost kissed me. "The nude room is open, Johnny," she said. "You're the best," I told her. She looked at me with her green eyes. "I get off at midnight," she whispered to me. "What's your number?" I asked her.

"Let's go!" Billy interrupted me and Daisy. "The nude room is open." "OK," I said to Billy and stared at Daisy again. Billy looked at John and saluted him. "Thanks for your patriotism, sir!" he said. John smiled at him and saluted back. "You Marines can change the world, and I hope you do," he told Billy.

Chapter 10 - Patriots versus Tyrants

For a people who are free and who mean to remain so, a well-organized and armed militia is their best security. -Thomas Jefferson

If there is one basic element in our Constitution, it is civilian control of the military. -Harry S. Truman

*****

A few days later Billy disappeared. I didn't know it until about a week later, when I drove over to his place to see if he was home. He didn't answer his cell phone for a week, so I went over to see him. His neighbor, a hot brunette with long legs, noticed me knocking on his door.

"Are you looking for Billy?" she asked. "Yes," I said. "He moved out a few days ago," she told me. "No one knows where he went, and he wouldn't talk to us when he was moving out . . . He was really quiet." "Are you a friend of his?" she asked. "Yeah," I said. "I'm just wondering where he moved to?" "No one knows . . . He was a cool dude," she smiled at me.

I told Jennifer about how Billy just moved away and didn't say a word about it. "Who knows?" she said, "Marines aren't exactly normal people." "He probably got a new job and moved away from Phoenix," she said. "I wish I'd met him, since he was your friend." "I don't know . . . It just seems strange to me," I told her. "Yeah, well Marines aren't exactly normal people, and you better find a new job," she told me.

About two months later I got a letter in the mail from Billy. He wrote that he burned his cell phone with gasoline and all his contacts from Phoenix. He said he, "Had enough of the bullshit in Phoenix," and being spied upon by the NSA. He said he moved into the mountains of Arizona. He said his girlfriend just got out of jail and was living with him. He invited me and Jennifer to his new place, and gave me directions.

I thought about his letter and decided to keep it quiet from Jennifer. I knew Jennifer was better off at home. About two weeks later, I drove out to visit Billy. It was a winding set of directions, but easy to follow. "Base MM-1?" is what I'm looking for, I laughed to myself. Billy said to follow the directions carefully and look for a "MM-1" sign, with an arrow off to the right of the road.

I couldn't believe it, but I found it. Base MM-1 was deep in the Arizona mountains, and a Marine was standing guard at the entrance. The place had heavy barbed-wire and concrete-barriers at the entrance. I slowly drove up to the guard-house. The Marine guard had an AR-10 rifle and full body armor.

"Are you lost? Do you need directions?" he asked me. "No, sir," I said, "I'm looking for Billy." The Marine looked at me hard and thought about it. "Yes, sir," he said, "I know that Jeep . . . Billy is expecting you," he nodded at me.

"I need you to shut-off your cell phone, take the battery out, and put it in this bag," he said. "It's a safety requirement for MM-1," he explained. "Anytime you want to make a phone call, just come back here and I'll give you your phone back." "No problem," I said, "You guys are smart." "Yes, sir," he answered.

I couldn't believe what I saw driving through the checkpoint. There were Marines all over the place and what appeared to be Army guys also. The place was a fortified compound in progress. There were Marines and Army guys walking around building bunkers made of sand-bags and cinder-blocks. They had a huge Caterpillar diesel tearing down trees and digging bunkers into the ground.

The road led to a bunch of Fifth-Wheel campers parked in the trees. This must be HQ, I thought to myself. I sat in the Jeep for a minute and waited. Then Billy came out of one of the campers. He was in Marine combat gear and welcomed me. "Good to see you, man," he said. "Yes, sir," I shook his hand. "Welcome to Marine Militia Base 1," he said. "MM-1?" I laughed, "I get it!"

"Where's Jennifer?" he asked. "I left her at home," I told him, "She doesn't like to party much." "Come on inside and meet my girlfriend," he said. "She just got out of jail." "Right on," I said, "This is incredible, what you've got going on up here in the mountains."

Billy nodded, "Yeah, I've had enough of the city and all the problems." "It's clean, fresh air up here . . . And what a view to kill for." "You wouldn't believe the wildlife up here."

Billy introduced me to his girlfriend, a good-looking redhead with big boobs. "I've heard a lot about you," she said, "I'm Rachel." "Good to meet you," I said back. "You want a beer?" Billy asked. "Hell, yeah," I answered, "Do you have any whiskey?" Billy laughed, "We've got all the beer and tequila you could want up here . . . We've got boxes of it."

"This is incredible," I said to him again, "What you're building up here." "Yeah, I've got a lot of Marine buddies from Iraq," he replied. "We all served in the Iraq War, and we've had enough of the Commie-Fascist government," he said. "The US government is so corrupt and evil it's not even funny," he became serious.

"Rachel just spent a year in jail for one marijuana cigarette," he said. "One harmless Mary Jane cigarette." "The government is fucked!" "I know," I said, "Mary Jane is beautiful like a flower, and it's also a medicine as well . . . It cures all sorts of medical problems." Rachel looked at me and smiled.

"You got a shot of tequila?" I asked Billy. Rachel handed me a pipe of Mary Jane instead. "I don't smoke," I told her. Billy laughed at me. "You want some tequila?" he laughed at me again. "We've got boxes of it . . . Crates and boxes of tequila and beer up here."

"I told you, I'm a Marine and know how to solve problems," he said drunkenly. "I got the fuck out of the city and moved up here for a reason," he said. "Take a shot, man," he went on. "Take a shot at the fucking New World Order," he told me. "You did some research at the library? Well, I did some research of my own," he said.

"Did you know George Washington conquered the British Navy with a platoon walking around without ammo in the dead of winter?" he asked. "Yes, sir," I nodded. "The British were the most powerful military ever known in 1776," he explained. "They had every advantage, every weapon, and all the money of the British empire to win against the American rebels."

"Yes, sir," I replied, "I know the Continental Army of Washington was broke and didn't stand a chance against the British in 1776." "That's right!" Billy looked me in the eyes. "But they had the American militia. Small-town people with big guns, who sniped British soldiers."

"Yes, sir," I answered, "The American militia were the worst nightmare of the British." "They would hide in trees and wage guerilla warfare against the British." "They would ambush British soldiers." "They were smart and didn't fuck-up."

"They won and turned the world upside down," Billy went

on. "That's what the beaten British said after losing," he said. "The world had been turned upside down." "God Bless America," I said to Billy, "So, what's the point?"

"The point is you're at Marine Militia Base 1," he answered. "This is MM-1." "This is just the first base of the Marine Militia movement." "Sure," I said, "Every American militia movement has been infiltrated by ATF agents, spies, and traitors selling fully-automatic weapons to idiots who don't know the laws."

"We know that and MM-1 will succeed," he said. "You want another beer?" he asked. "Yeah," I said, "I also know the American militia were more powerful than the Continental Army of enlisted men under Washington." "The worst nightmare the British faced were the American rebels. They were volunteers who came and went, serving the towns and cities against the evil British troops." "The civilian militia won the war."

"That's right," Billy nodded, "The militia were more powerful than the enlisted Continental Army." "They would snipe British officials and then disappear into the country." "They would hide in the hills and randomly attack British troops." "They waged what was called guerrilla warfare against the British . . . And they won." "Yes, sir," I said.

I took another shot and walked outside into the cool mountain air. The sun had gone down, and I saw the first star of the night. These people are crazy, I thought to myself. It's just like Jennifer said, Marines are not normal people. I shook my head thinking about it, and went back inside the camper. Billy was slamming tequila at this point, and he was drunk out of his mind.

"Guess what?" he asked. "I don't know?" I answered. "We've got a bunch of Army veterans we signed up . . . Not just me and my buddies," he said. "Those are the guys building the bunkers and securing the perimeter." "We all pitched in our Iraq war-cash and have a Caterpillar tearing down trees and building a base." "Yeah," I said, "I noticed that."

"God Bless America," I said, "Maybe the Marine Militia can save us?" "Maybe the Marine Militia can save our freedoms and liberties?" "We're not gonna save you," Billy answered. "You're gonna save yourselves." "How?" I asked him. "You're the Civilian Corps. branch of the Marine Militia," he answered. "You're the most powerful branch of MM-1."

"Patriotic civilians like you are the answer," he explained. "You're a true patriot, whether you realize it or not." "We, Marines, and veterans will do the heavy-lifting to restore freedom and liberty, but you civilians are what matters." "We need every man, woman, and child in America to join us."

"What about the NSA spy satellites turned upon America?" I asked him. "They can see us and hear us right now in this camper?" "They're spying on us in real-time." "Fuck the spy satellites!" Billy shouted, "All we have to do is pull the plug on the big computer in the sky!" "We, Marines, know how to deal with enemy surveillance."

I thought about it and agreed with him. "Maybe we should protest in Phoenix against the NSA?" I asked him. "Protest? Protest against what?" he answered. "Protest against the senile politicians in Washington, DC?" "Protest against the traitors who run the NSA?"

"Yeah, protesting is a waste of time against the old people and politicians," I agreed with him. "What's the point of being rounded-up in downtown Phoenix by the *Intelligence Police*?" Billy looked at me seriously, "These people are traitors!" "They're not *Real Americans!*"

Billy laughed, "Smart Americans are moving to the country, buying AR-10's, lots of ammo, and big diesel trucks." "The evil Commie-Fascist government doesn't stand a chance against us!" Billy yelled, "Semper Fi!"

Just then someone knocked on the door of the camper. Billy looked out the window and opened the door. "Hey, Clint," he said, "Come on in, what's up?" Clint saluted him and said, "We just got some intel on the radio." "It's no big deal, but the neighbor's are wondering about the traffic in and out of here."

No way, I thought to myself. It's Clint Franco. He had a military radio and Navy SEAL combat gear on. "Clint Franco?" I said to him, "What are you doing up here at MM-1?" He looked at me for a second and then laughed, "Johnny Page!"

He shook my hand with a firm grip, like he used to do at Telcore USA. "You guys know each other?" Billy was surprised. "Hell, yeah, we know each other," I said. "This guy is a Navy SEAL and telecommunications expert."

"That's what he told us when he joined MM-1," Billy said.

I looked Clint in the eyes, "But, you're with The Company?" I asked him. "You're a Company man." "Fuck the NSA!" Clint replied, "I told them to fuck-off and stop spying on my wife and kids."

"I'm not an NSA traitor inside the government." "I swore an Oath to defend the Constitution from all enemies, and that includes the NSA." "Yes, sir," Billy saluted him drunkenly. "The fuckers were spying on me, my wife, and even our kids," Clint explained.

"So, you know about the military satellites turned upon the American people?" I asked him. Clint shook his head sadly. "Hell, I helped them build the goddamned robot in the sky," he answered.

"When they start spying on your wife and kids," he paused and thought about it, "It draws a line in the sand." "It crossed a line for me and I told them to fuck-off." "Fuck the NSA!" Clint said.

"Can the intel wait until tomorrow?" Billy asked Clint. "Yes, sir," Clint answered. "We're sort of partying right now," Billy said. "I'll brief you in the morning," Clint replied and saluted him again. "Good to see you again," I told Clint and shook his hand.

Billy handed me the tequila. "Now, take an Oath to the 1776 Constitution of the United States," he said. Rachel started laughing at Billy. "OK," I said, "I actually know the Pledge of Allegiance," I told him. "You're the first member of the Civilian Corps of the Marine Militia," Billy smiled at me.

"Do it!" Rachel laughed and took a shot of tequila. "Pledge Allegiance to 1776 America!" "I pledge Allegiance to the Flag of 1776 America," I said. "No, that's not it," Rachel laughed, "You got it wrong." "OK," I said, "Maybe I can do this in the morning." "Yeah," she was laughing, "That's fine."

"I'm so wasted," Billy said to Rachel, "Give me another shot." "Take another shot Johnny . . . Here's to 1776 America!" "To 1776 America!" Rachel laughed and took another shot. We all passed out drunk and stoned a few hours later after jamming the Rolling Stones and Beatles on the 1,000 watt Hi-Fi stereo.

At high noon the next day, Billy and some Marines had me pledge an Oath to the 1776 Constitution of the United States. Billy said I was the first member of the Marine Militia Civilian

Corps. He told me to go back to Phoenix and buy a good .308 rifle, lots of ammo, and all the military gear I could round-up. He told me to come back in a week and bring Jennifer with me.

"OK," I said, "I see what you're doing up here in the mountains." "I like it and I think it's righteous, man." "You think the Marine Militia can shut-down the NSA spy satellites?" I asked him. "That's the key to the illegal spying on Americans -- The satellites they're using against the American People?"

Billy looked at me hard and thought about it. "We conquered Iwo Jima . . . We conquered the beaches of Normandy," he replied. "We're the Marines, and we will protect the Sacred Fire of Liberty." I nodded at Billy, "Yeah, the Sacred Fire of Liberty . . . That's what George Washington called it."

"We're gonna take back freedom and liberty and restore it to 1776," Billy said. "The Founding Father's told us what to do and were gonna do it." "We're not stupid up here," he went on, "We're not gonna be infiltrated by ATF agents, and we're not hiding in old railroad tunnels either."

"We know we're being spied upon with military satellites," Billy looked up at the sky. "OK," I said, "Give me a few weeks or so, and I'll be back with Jennifer." I shook his hand. As I was leaving, Rachel ran up to us. "Look up at the sky, and what do you see?" I asked her. "It's a blue sky, and the sun is shining . . . It's a nice day," she laughed. "Look, I found a mountain flower."

"The NSA is spying on us right now with satellites," I told her. "You can't see them in daylight, but the stars and satellites are above us -- Just like at night." "They can see us, hear us, and they're recording our lives into a NSA satellite database."

Rachel looked at me and suddenly became sad. "That's so evil," she said. "I'm only 25-years-old and I want to live in a free country!" "This is America! A free country!" "The American people have a right to freedom and privacy!" she said.

"It's not a free country anymore," I told her. "There's a gang of traitors in Washington, DC -- And they hate freedom, liberty, and privacy." "There's an NSA spy machine inside the government." "The old politicians are keeping it a secret, and they're hiding it from the American people."

Rachel looked at Billy and said, "Sounds like a job for the Marines." Billy told her, "We're gonna pull the plug on those NSA spy satellites," he said. "Don't you worry about it . . . Death to Tyrants." "Live Free or Die," I said back to Billy. "Liberty or Death," Billy replied. As I drove away, Rachel took off running into the forest, half-naked on a beautiful sunny day.

Made in United States
Troutdale, OR
02/12/2025